English Made Easy

Learning English Through Pictures

VOLUME ONE

By Jonathan Crichton and Pieter Koster

TUTTLE PUBLISHING
Tokyo • Rutland, Vermont • Singapore

Published by Tuttle Publishing, an imprint of Periplus Editions (HK) Ltd.,
with editorial offices at 364 Innovation Drive, North Clarendon, Vermont 05759 U.S.A.
and 130 Joo Seng Road #06-01, Singapore 368357.

ISBN-13: 978-0-8048-3736-1
ISBN-10: 0-8048-3736-8
IBSN-13: 978-4-8053-0862-2 (for sale in Japan only)
ISBN 4-8053-0862-1 (for sale in Japan only)

Distributed by:

North America, Latin America & Europe
Tuttle Publishing
364 Innovation Drive, North Clarendon,
VT 05759-9436 U.S.A.
Tel: 1 (802) 773-8930
Fax: 1 (802) 773-6993
info@tuttlepublishing.com
www.tuttlepublishing.com

Japan
Tuttle Publishing
Yaekari Building, 3rd Floor, 5-4-12 Osaki, Shinagawa-ku
Tokyo 141-0032
Tel: (81) 3 5437-0171
Fax: (81) 3 5437-0755
tuttle-sales@gol.com

Asia Pacific
Berkeley Books Pte. Ltd.
130 Joo Seng Road #06-01, Singapore 368357
Tel: (65) 6280-1330
Fax: (65) 6280-6290
inquiries@periplus.com.sg
www.periplus.com

11 10 09 08 07   6 5 4 3 2

Printed in Singapore

TUTTLE PUBLISHING® is a registered trademark of Tuttle Publishing, a division of Periplus Editions (HK) Ltd.

Contents

FUNCTION	GRAMMAR	VOCABULARY

FUNCTION	GRAMMAR	VOCABULARY

Preface

In an increasingly international world, being able to communicate in English is nowadays a necessity in social, professional and business life. Competence in English creates an increasing range of business, travel and leisure opportunities, opening doors to international communication.

English Made Easy is a breakthrough in English language learning – imaginatively exploiting how pictures and text can work together to create understanding and help learners learn more productively.

English Made Easy gives learners easy access to the vocabulary, grammar and functions of English as it is actually used in a comprehensive range of social situations. Self-guided students and classroom learners alike will be delighted by the way they are helped to progress easily from one unit to the next, using the combinations of pictures and text to discover for themselves how English works.

The *English Made Easy* method is based on a thorough understanding of language structure and how language is successfully learned. The authors are experienced English language teachers with strong backgrounds in language analysis and language learning. The *English Made Easy* team is confident that the books represent a significant development in English language learning.

— Professor Christopher N. Candlin

Using this book

This book is easy to use. You will learn how to speak English by looking at the pictures and words on each page. The pictures explain the words.

The table of contents tells you what you will learn in each of the twenty units. You can use this table to look up any particular points you want to learn or practice.

The twenty units are arranged in groups of five. The first four units present language and give you opportunities to practice as you learn. The first page of each unit has a list of all the words and phrases you will learn in that unit, together with a pronunciation guide. At the end of each unit there is an interesting story which uses the language you have just learned.

The fifth unit in each group gives you the opportunity to revise the language in the first four units and to use it in different situations. The exercises are easy to understand and there is an answer key at the end of the unit.

At the end of the book there is an index which contains all the words and phrases in the book. It is not a dictionary. It refers you to the unit in which that language first appears so that you can 'discover' the meaning of the word by seeing it in context.

a [ei, ə]
the [ðə]

book [buk]
camera [kæm'ərə]
car [ka:r]
house [haus]
key [ki:]
laptop [læp'ta:p]
mobile phone [moub'əl foun]
pen [pen]
purse [pə:rs]
wallet [wa:l'it]
watch [wa:tʃ]

whose [hu:z]

her [hə:r]
his [hiz]
my [mai]
our [au'ə:r]
their [ðe:r]
your [ju:r]

My name's ... [mai neimz]
What's your name? [wʌts ju:r neim]

yes [jes]
no [nou]
I don't know. [ai dount nou]

family [fæm'li:]

husband [hʌz'bənd]
wife [waif]

father [fa:'ðə:r]
mother [mʌð'ə:r]

son [sʌn]
daughter [dɔ:t'ə:r]

brother [brʌð'ə:r]
sister [sis'tə:r]

name [neim]

is [iz]
isn't [iz'ənt]

it [it]
this [ðis]
what [wʌt]

this is [ðis iz]
it's [its]

Excuse me. [eksku:z' mi:]
Thank you. [θæŋk ju:]

The Benson Family

1

2

3

4

1

This is his father.

2

This is her father.

3

This is their father.

4

This is his mother.

5

This is her mother.

6

This is their mother.

it is = it's   is not = isn't

1

a book

2

This is my book.

3

This isn't my book. It's your book.

4

This isn't my book. It's your book.

5

Thank you.

Thank you.

do not = don't

1 This isn't my book. It isn't your book. It's Tom's book.

2 It's his book.

3 This isn't my book. It isn't your book. It's Anne's book.

4 It's her book.

5 Whose book is this?

6 I don't know.

1 a camera	**2** a mobile phone	**3** a key	**4** a pen	**5** a house
6 cameras	**7** mobile phones	**8** keys	**9** pens	**10** houses
11 a laptop	**12** a watch	**13** a wallet	**14** a purse	**15** a car
16 laptops	**17** watches	**18** wallets	**19** purses	**20** cars

The Bensons

UNIT 2: That'd be great!

art gallery [a:rt gæl'ə:ri:]

beach [bi:tʃ]

concert [ka:n'sə:rt]

dinner [din'ə:r]

lunch [lʌntʃ]

meeting [mi:'tiŋ]

movies [mu:'vɪ:z]

picnic [pik'nik]

party [pa:r'ti:]

restaurant [res'tə:rənt]

theater [θi:'ətə:r]

market [ma:r'kit]

bring [briŋ]

bringing [briŋ'iŋ]

can [kæn]

come [kʌm]

coming [kʌm'iŋ]

go [gou]

going [gou'iŋ]

take [teik]

taking [teik'iŋ]

know [nou]

How about...? [hau əbaut']

let's [lets]

Would you like to come to... ?

[wud ju: laik tu: kʌm tu:]

Sure. [ʃu:r]

I'd love to. [aid lʌv tu:]

That'd be great. [ðæ'təd bi:greit]

OK. [oukei']

I'd love to but I can't. [aid lʌv tu: bʌt ai kænt]

I'm afraid I can't. [aim əfreid' ai kænt]

Sorry, I can't. [sa:r'i: ai kænt]

door [dɔ:r]

enter [en'tə:r]

exit [eg'zit]

in [in]

out [aut]

to [tu:]

am [æm]

are [a:r]

who [hu:]

but [bʌt]

I [ai]

you [ju:]

he [hi:]

she [ʃi:]

we [wi:]

they [ðei]

me [mi:]

you [ju:]

him [him]

her [hə:r]

us [ʌs]

them [ðem]

who is = who's

I am = I'm   **he is** = he's

they are = they're   **we are** = we're   **she is** = she's

Would you like to come to... ?

1  the movies	**2**  dinner	**3**  lunch
4  the beach	**5**  a picnic	**6**  a party
7  a concert	**8**  a market	**9**  a meeting
10  a restaurant	**11**  the theater	**12**  an art gallery

The Bensons

UNIT 3: I'd like you to meet my accountant.

meet   [mi:t]

met   [met]

accountant   [əkaun'tənt]

colleague   [ka:l'i:g]

friend   [frend]

teacher   [ti:tʃə:r]

manager   [mæn'idʒə:r]

neighbor   [neib'ə:r]

secretary   [sek'ri:te:ri:]

Have you met...?   [hæv ju: met]

I'd like you to meet...   [aid laik ju: tu: mi:t]

Hi. [ ]

No, I haven't.   [nou ai hæv'ənt]

Good to meet you.   [gud tu: mi:t ju:]

here   [hi:r]

that   [ðæt]

there   [ðe:r]

these   [ði:z]

those   [ðouz]

where   [we:r]

looks like   [luks laik]

I'd like   [aid laik]

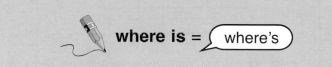 

where is = where's   that is = that's

27

I'd like you to meet ...

1

my wife Peggy.

2

my son Tom.

3

my neighbor John.

4

my secretary Janice.

5

my accountant Henry.

6

my manager Mr. Lee.

7

Anne's friend Judy.

8

Tom's teacher Mrs Cooper.

9

my colleague David.

1

Alan, I'd like you to meet my manager Mr. Lee. Mr Lee, this is my friend Alan.

2

Hi.

Good to meet you.

3

Alan, I'd like you to meet my colleague David. David, this is my friend Alan.

4

Hi.

Good to meet you.

5

....
....

6

....
....

....
....

29

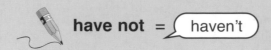

have not = haven't

Jim, have you met my friend Alex?

No, I haven't. Good to meet you Alex.

....
....

....
....

The Bensons

not [nɑ:t]

aren't [a:rnt]

doesn't [dʌz'nt]

don't [dɒunt]

isn't [iz'ənt]

does [dʌz]

do [du:]

fit [fit]

looks good [luks gud]

runs [rʌnz]

play [ɒlei]

work [wə:rk]

sit [sit]

beautiful [bju:'təfəl]

cold [kould]

cute [kju:t]

fast [fæst]

good [gud]

great [greit]

hot [hɑ:t]

wet [wet]

well [wel]

lovely [lʌv'li:]

baby [bei'bi:]

day [dei]

shoes [ʃu:z]

view [vju:]

plane [plein]

seat [si:t]

mine [main]

yours [ju:rz]

It's all right. [its ɔ:l rait]

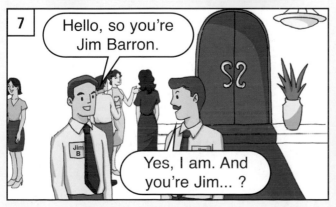

they are = they're

35

1

2

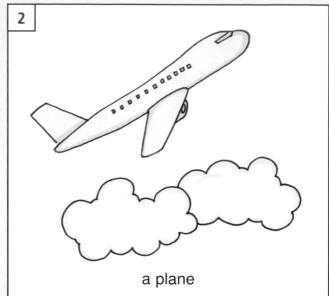

a plane

3

4

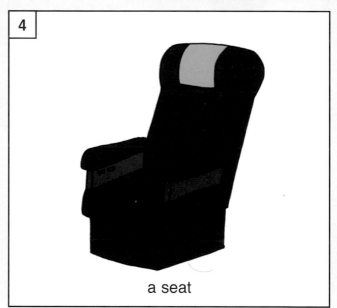

a seat

5

6

1

a beautiful day...

2

wet...

3

hot...

4

cold...

5

a great party...

6

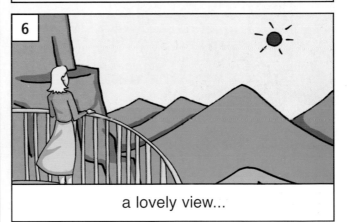

a lovely view...

7

a good camera...

8

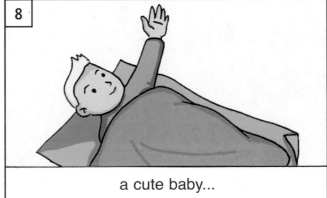

a cute baby...

isn't it?

Yes, it is.

does not = doesn't.

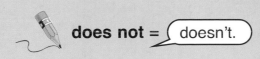

1

He runs fast, doesn't he?
Yes, he does.

2

It looks good, doesn't it?
Yes, it does.

3

Yes, they do.
They play well, don't they?
No, they don't.

4

You look like your brother, don't you?
Yes, I do.

5

Those shoes don't fit, do they?
No, they don't.

6

This camera doesn't work, does it?
No, it doesn't.

The Bensons

UNIT 5: Revision and extension

1
.............book.............

2
....

3
....

4
....

5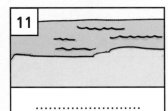
....

6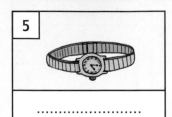
....

7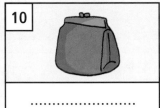
....

8
....

9
....

10
....

11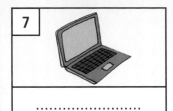
....

12
....

13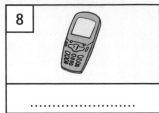
....

14
....

15
....

16
....

17
....

18
....

19
....

20
....

21 	**22** 	**23** 	**24**  ....
25 	**26** 	**27** 	**28**  ....
29 JIM BENSON	**30** 	**31** 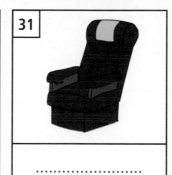	**32**  ....
33 	**34** 	**35** 	**36**  ....
37 	**38** 	**39** 	**40**  ....

A

1. What's your name?

2. Whose book is this?

3. Would you like to come to my party?

4. Thank you.

5. Where's my book?

6. This is my brother Kim.

a. That's OK.

b. Good to meet you.

c. Tom.

d. It's her book.

e. Here.

f. Yes, I'd love to.

B

1. Are you Jim Benson?

2. Is your name Jim Benson?

3. These are your books, aren't they?

4. He is your father, isn't he?

5. She is your sister, isn't she?

a. Yes, he is.

b. Yes, she is.

c. Yes, it is.

d. Yes, they are.

e. Yes, I am.

C

1. He runs fast, doesn't he?

2. This camera doesn't work, does it?

3. These shoes don't fit, do they?

4. You look like your brother, don't you?

a. Yes, he does.

b. No, they don't.

c. Yes, I do.

d. No, it doesn't.

this	Come	isn't	mine	his	isn't it

1 Is ...this... your wallet?

No, it .... mine.

2 It's ....

OK, thanks.

3 .... in.

4 This is your wallet, ... ?

No, it isn't.

5 It's .... Thank you.

6

yours	your	it's	mine	it isn't	Whose	this

1

Tom, is this ...your... pen?

2

No, ... his.

3

This is .... , isn't it?

No, ...

4

.... pen is .... ?

5

It's ....

6

46

it is	your	like to	meet	My	isn't it

1

It's cold, ...isn't... ..it.. ?

Yes, ...

2

.... name's Peggy.

Good to .... you.
My name's Barbara.

3

What's .... name?

Tom.

4

Would you ....
.... sit here?

Yes, please.

47

Yes   about   can't   I am   Good   haven't

1

Hello.

Hi.

2

You're Penny, aren't you?

Yes, ...am......

3

Have you met Penny?

No, I ....
.... to meet you.

4

I'm Anne. It's a beautiful day, isn't it?

.... , it is.

5

Let's have lunch here.

Sorry, I ....

6

How ....
going to a movie?

Yes, OK.

OK.

➤ restaurant go a Let's to

➤ OK

➤ come like to you Would to lunch

➤ can't afraid I'm I Sorry

➤ met neighbor you my Have

➤ haven't No I

➤ meet to Jane like I'd you

➤ meet you to Good

➤ movie to going about How a

➤ great be That'd

➤ going You're to the meeting aren't you

➤ I'm No not

1

➤ book It's interesting an isn't it

➤ it Yes is

2

➤ good This looks laptop doesn't it

➤ does Yes it

3

➤ pen my That's isn't it

➤ isn't No it

4

➤ are keys yours These aren't they

➤ Yes are they

5

➤ here work You don't you

➤ No I don't

6

➤ concerts like You don't you

➤ do I Yes

UNIT 5: Answers

Unit 5, page 42

1. book	2. camera	3. car	4. family	5. watch
6. house	7. laptop	8. mobile phone	9. pen	10. purse
11. beach	12. key	13. art gallery	14. dinner	15. market
16. lunch	17. meeting	18. theater	19. party	20. restaurant

Unit 5, page 43

21. accountant	22. colleague	23. friend	24. manager	25. neighbor
26. secretary	27. teacher	28. baby	29. name	30. plane
31. seat	32. cold	33. shoes	34. view	35. wet
36. hot	37. movies	38. door	39. wallet	40. concert

Unit 5, page 44

A. 1c 2d 3f 4a 5e 6b   B. 1e 2c 3d 4a 5b   C. 1a 2d 3b 4c

Unit 5, page 45

1. this, isn't   2. his   3. Come   4. isn't it   5. mine

Unit 5, page 46

1. your   2. it's   3. yours? it isn't   4. Whose, this   5. mine

Unit 5, page 47

1. isn't it, it is   2. My, meet   3. your   4. like to

Unit 5, page 48

2. I am   3. haven't, Good   4. Yes   5. can't   6. about

Unit 5, page 49

1. Let's go to a restaurant.
   OK.

2. Would you like to come to lunch?
   Sorry, I'm afraid I can't.

3. Have you met my neighbor?
   No, I haven't.

4. I'd like you to meet Jane.
   Good to meet you.

5. How about going to a movie?
   That'd be great.

6. You're going to the meeting,
   aren't you?
   No, I'm not.

Unit 5, page 50

1. It's an interesting book, isn't it?
   Yes, it is.

2. This laptop looks good, doesn't it?
   Yes, it does.

3. That's my pen, isn't it?
   No, it isn't.

4. These keys are yours, aren't they?
   Yes, they are.

5. You work here, don't you?
   No, I don't.

6. You like concerts, don't you?
   Yes, I do.

UNIT 6: Would you like something to drink?

Would you like...? [wud ju: laik]
What would you like? [wa:t wud ju: laik]

No, thanks. [nou θæŋks]
Yes, please. [jes pli:z]
...would be nice. [wud bi: nais]

something to eat [sʌm'θiŋ tu: i:t]
piece of... [pi:s ʌv]
something to drink [sʌm'θiŋ tu: driŋk]
cup of... [kʌp ʌv]
glass of... [glæs ʌv]
can of... [kæn ʌv]
bottle of... [ba:t'əl ʌv]

cookie [kuk'i:]
chips [tʃips]
sausage [sɔ:'sidʒ]
nuts [nʌts]
cake [keik]

sandwich [sænd'witʃ]
burger [bə:r'gə:r]

juice [dʒu:s]
milk [milk]
water [wɔ:'tə:r]
tea [ti:]
coffee [kɔ:f'i:]
sugar [ʃug'ə:r]

apple [æp'əl]
banana [bənæn'ə]
peach [pi:tʃ]
orange [ɔ:r'indʒ]
plum [plʌm]
pear [pe:r]

How many... ? [hou meni:]

one [wʌn]
two [tu:]
three [θri:]
four [fɔ:r]
five [faiv]
six [siks]
seven [sev'ən]
eight [eit]
nine [nain]
ten [ten]

bag [bæg]
child [tʃaild]
tablet [tæb'let]
ticket [tik'ət]
sock [sa:k]

a pair of [ə pe:r ʌv]
some [sʌm]

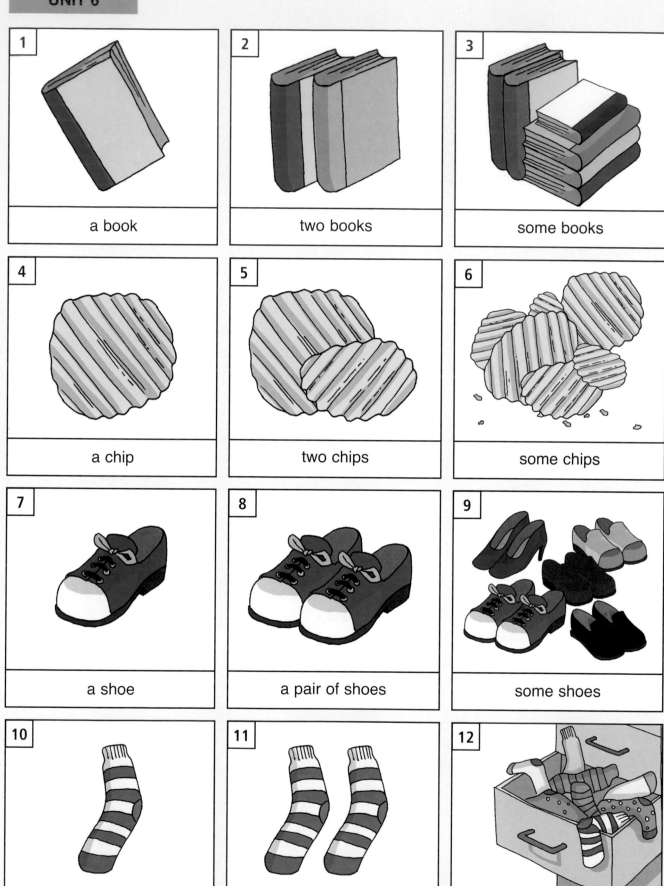

1 a book	**2** two books	**3** some books
4 a chip	**5** two chips	**6** some chips
7 a shoe	**8** a pair of shoes	**9** some shoes
10 a sock	**11** a pair of socks	**12** some socks

Would you like...?

1

some chips

2
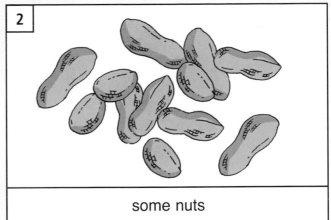
some nuts

3

a sausage

4

a cookie

5
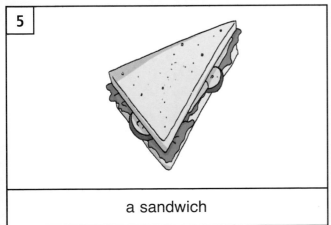
a sandwich

6

a burger

something to eat

 Yes, please.

No, thanks.

Would you like...?

1

an apple

2

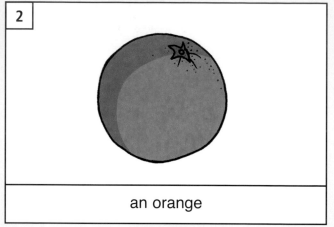

an orange

3

a banana

4

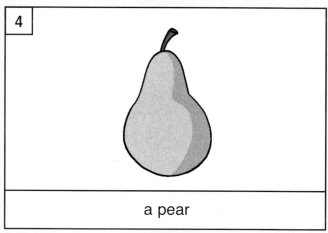

a pear

5

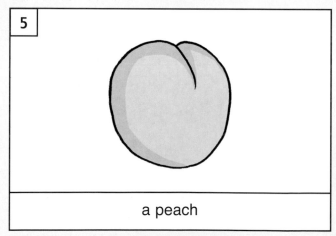

a peach

6

a plum

something to eat

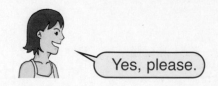

Yes, please.

No, thanks.

Would you like...?

1  a can of Fizzo	**2**  a bottle of orange juice
3  a glass of water	**4**  a glass of milk
5  a cup of tea	**6**  a cup of coffee

something to drink

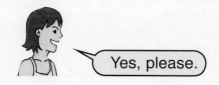 Yes, please.

 No, thanks.

1

Would you like something to drink?

Yes, please.

2

What would you like?

A glass of water would be nice.

3

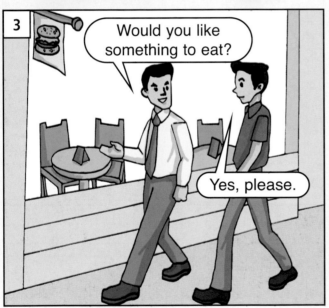

Would you like something to eat?

Yes, please.

4

What would you like?

A sandwich would be nice.

5

.... something to eat?

Yes, please.

6

What ....

An apple, please.

1 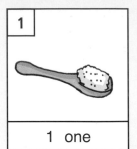	**2** 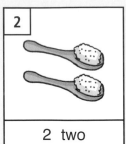	**3** 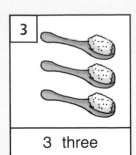	**4** 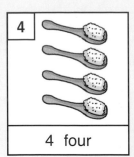	**5** 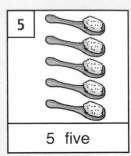
1 one	2 two	3 three	4 four	5 five

6

Sugar?

Yes, please.

7

How many?

Two, please.

8 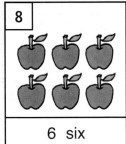	**9** 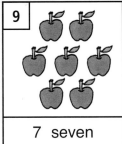	**10** 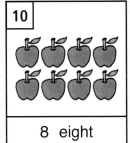	**11** 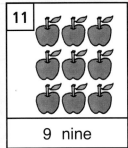	**12** 
6 six	7 seven	8 eight	9 nine	10 ten

13

Apples?

Yes.

14

How many?

Six.

1

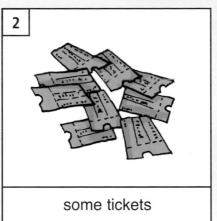

a ticket

2

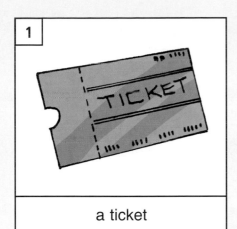

some tickets

3

How many tickets?

Three, please.

4

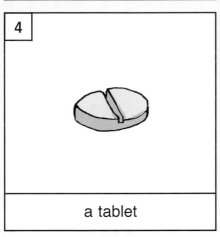

a tablet

5

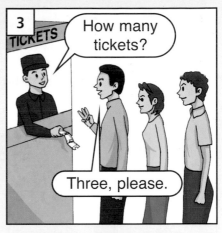

some tablets

6

How many tablets?

One.

7

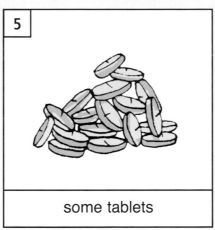

a child

8

some children

9

How many children?

Five.

10

a bag

11

some bags

12

How many bags?

Four.

The Bensons

UNIT 7: He's a tour guide.

application form [æplikei′ʃən fɔ:rm]

occupation [a:kjəpei′ʃən]

businessman [biz′nismæn]

pharmacist [fa:r′məsist]

doctor [da:k′tə:r]

nurse [nə:rs]

mechanic [məkæn′ik]

police officer [pəli:s′ ɔ:f′isə:r]

receptionist [risep′ʃənist]

sales assistant [seilz əsis′tənt]

taxi driver [tæk′si: drai′və:r]

tour guide [tu:r gaid]

now [nau]

too [tu:]

from [frʌm]

to [tu:]

hello [heloú]

hi [hai]

What do you do? [wʌt du: ju: du:]

I'm a ... [aim ə]

did [did]

was [wʌz]

were [wə:r]

when [wen]

have [hæv]

How many ... do you have?

[hau men′i: du: ju: hæv]

Could you repeat that, please?

[kud ju: ripi:t′ ðæt pli:z]

I'm sorry. [aim sa:r′i:]

slowly [sloúli:]

a taxi

a taxi driver

What's your name?

John Phillips.

What do you do?

I'm a taxi driver.

APPLICATION FORM

NAME: John Phillips

OCCUPATION: taxi driver

1

My name's Kerry. I'm a pharmacist.

2

My name's Phil. I'm a mechanic.

3
My name's Gerry. I'm a nurse.

4

My name's Brad. I'm a businessman.

5

My name's Marge. I'm a doctor.

6

My name's Vivien. I'm a receptionist.

7

My name's Jeff. I'm a police officer.

8

My name's Alison. I'm a teacher.

9

That's my neighbor. He's a tour guide.

10

That's my friend. He's a sales assistant.

That's my sister. She's a sales assistant, too.

66

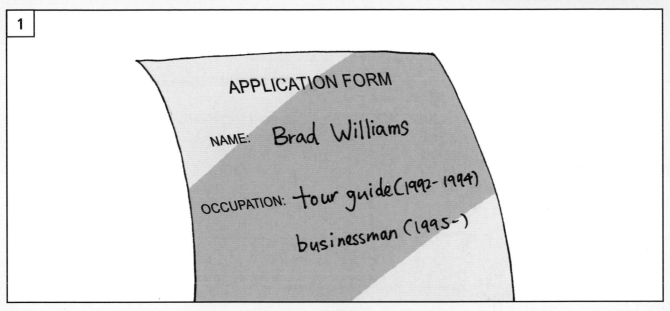

1

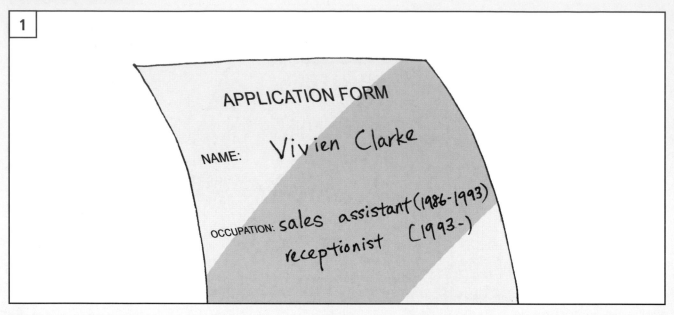

2

3

4

69

The Bensons

UNIT 8: I'm going to New York.

How did you get here?
[hau did ju: get hi:r]

How long have you been here?
[hau lɔ:ŋ hæv ju: bin hi:r]

I'm from... [aim frʌm]

I've been here for... [aiv bin hi:r fɔ:r]

Where are you from? [we:r a:r ju: frʌm]

arrive [əraiv']

leave [li:v]

January [dʒæn'ju:we:ri:]

February [feb'jəwe:ri:]

March [ma:rtʃ]

April [eip'rəl]

May [mei]

June [dʒu:n]

July [dʒʌlai']

August [ɔ:g'əst]

September [septem'bə:r]

October [a:ktoʊbə:r]

November [nouvem'bə:r]

December [disem'bə:r]

eleven [ilev'ən]

twelve [twelv]

thirteen [θə:r'ti:n']

fourteen [fɔ:r'ti:n']

fifteen [fif'ti:n']

sixteen [siks'ti:n']

seventeen [sev'ənti:n']

eighteen [ei'ti:n']

nineteen [nain'ti:n']

twenty [twen'ti:]

everyone [ev'ri:wʌn]

Monday [mʌn'dei]

Tuesday [tu:z'dei]

Wednesday [wenz'dei]

Thursday [θə:rz'dei]

Friday [frai'dei]

Saturday [sæt'ə:rdei]

Sunday [sʌn'dei]

month [mʌnθ]

week [wi:k]

weekend [wi:k'end]

year [ji:r]

day [dei]

How much... ? [hau mʌtʃ]

dollars [da:l'ə:rz]

cents [sents]

school [sku:l]

by [bai]

since [sins]

for [fɔ:r]

still [stil]

bus [bʌs]

plane [plein]

train [trein]

1

$

dollars

¢

cents

2

How much is this pen?

It's eleven dollars.

= $11

3

How much is this wallet?

It's twelve dollars.

= $12

4

How much is that book?

It's thirteen dollars.

= $13

5

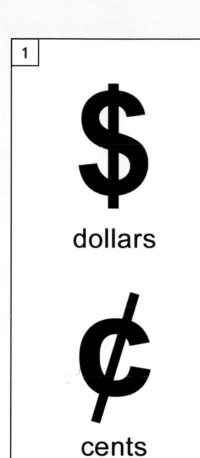

How much is that purse?

It's fourteen dollars.

= $14

6

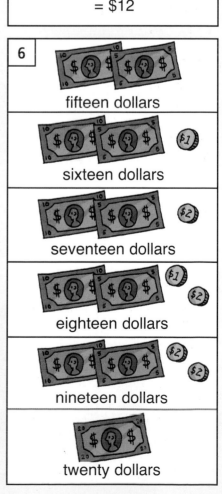

fifteen dollars

sixteen dollars

seventeen dollars

eighteen dollars

nineteen dollars

twenty dollars

1

2

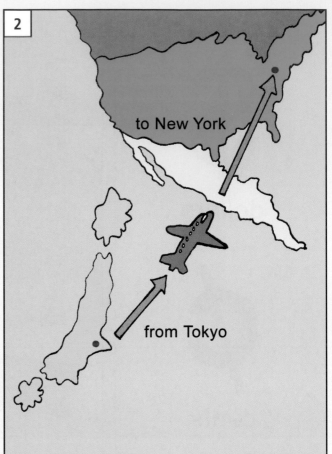

to New York

from Tokyo

3

Where are you from?

I'm from Tokyo.

4 I'm from Paris.

5 I'm from Sydney.

6 We're from Moscow.

7 We're from Cairo.

8 I'm from London.

1

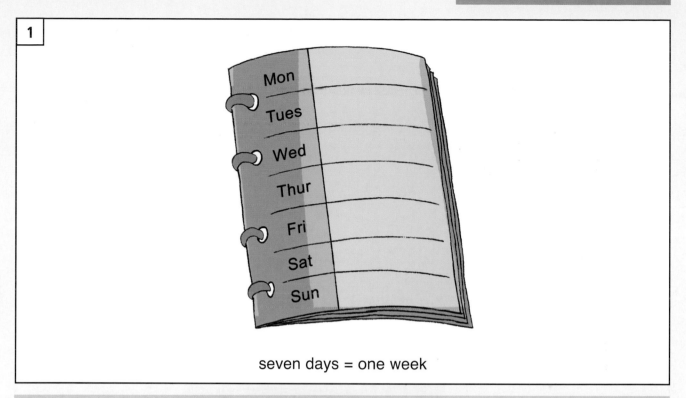

seven days = one week

Mon	Tues	Wed	Thurs	Fri	Sat	Sun
Monday	Tuesday	Wednesday	Thursday	Friday	Saturday	Sunday
					Weekend	

2

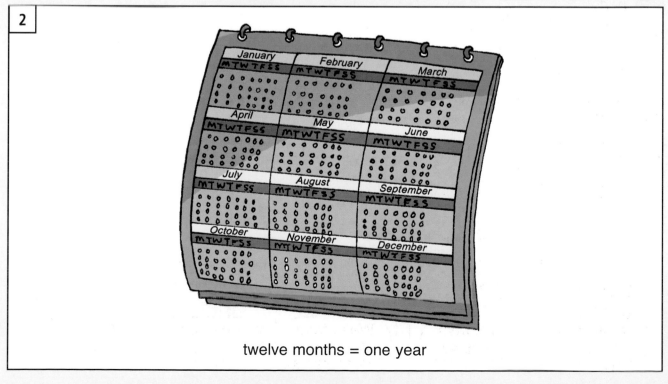

twelve months = one year

I have = I've   we have = we've

Monday

> How long have you been here?

> I've been here for two days.

Wednesday

Saturday 4th October

> How long have you been here?

> We've been here for two weeks.

Saturday 18th October

June 10th

> How long have you been here?

> ....
> ....

December 10th

1 Airport

1996, Australia

2

How long have you been in Australia?

For three years.

Since 1996.

1999

3

How did you get here?

By plane.

4

August, Sydney

5

How long have you been in Sydney?

For two months.

Since August.

October

6

How did you get here?

By train.

7

Wednesday, Sydney

8

How long have you been in Sydney?

....
....

....

Saturday

9

How did you get here?

By bus.

The Bensons

rice [rais]

bread [bred]

potato [pətei′tou]

pasta [pa:s′tə]

peas [pi:z]

onion [ʌn′jən]

carrot [kær′ət]

tomato [təmei′tou]

beans [bi:nz]

cauliflower [kɔ:′leflauə:r]

cabbage [kæb′idʒ]

broccoli [bra:k′əli:]

cucumber [kju:′kʌmbə:r]

lettuce [let′is]

mushroom [mʌʃ′ru:m]

ice cream [ais kri:m]

big [big]

small [smɔ:l]

boring [bɔ:r′iŋ]

interesting [in′tristiŋ]

cheap [tʃi:p]

expensive [ikspen′siv]

tall [tɔ:l]

short [ʃɔ:rt]

heavy [he′vi:]

light [lait]

wide [waid]

narrow [nær′ou]

good [gud]

bad [bæd]

bigger [bi′gə:r]

smaller [smɔ:′lə:r]

more boring [mɔ:r bɔ:r′iŋ]

more interesting [mɔ:r in′tristiŋ]

cheaper [tʃi:′pə:r]

more expensive [mɔ:r ikspen′siv]

taller [tɔ:′lə:r]

shorter [ʃɔ:rt′ə:r]

heavier [he′vi:ə:r]

lighter [lait′ə:r]

wider [waid′ə:r]

narrower [nær′ouə:r]

better [bet′ə:r]

worse [wə:rs]

biggest [bi′gist]

smallest [smɔ:′list]

most boring [moust bɔ:r′iŋ]

most interesting [moust in′tristiŋ]

cheapest [tʃi:′pist]

most expensive [moust ikspen′siv]

tallest [tɔ:′list]

shortest [ʃɔ:rt′ist]

heaviest [he′vi:ist]

lightest [lait′ist]

widest [waid′ist]

narrowest [nær′ouist]

best [best]

worst [wə:rst]

---

very [ve:r′i:]

very much [ve:r′i: mʌtʃ]

What do you think? [wʌt du: ju: θiŋk]

Do you like... ? [du: ju: laik]

Can I help you? [kæn ai help ju:]

---

agree [əgri:′]

think [θiŋk]

like [laik]

suitcase [su:t′keis]

pair of sunglasses [pe:r ʌv sʌn′glæsiz]

cap [kæp]

surfboard [sə:rf′bɔ:rd]

basketball player [bæs′kitbɔ:l plei′ə:r]

jockey [dʒa:k′i:]

horse [hɔ:rs]

pants [pænts]

Do you like...?

1  bread	2 potatoes	3 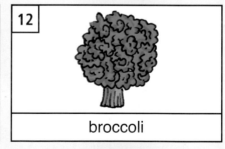 rice
4  pasta	5  onions	6 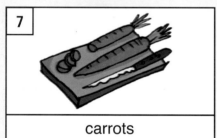 peas
7 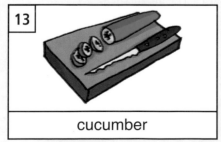 carrots	8 tomatoes	9  beans
10  cauliflower	11  cabbage	12 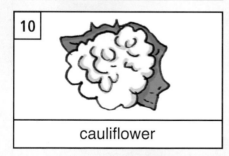 broccoli
13  cucumber	14 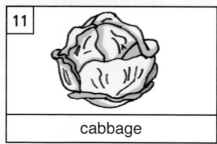 lettuce	15  mushrooms

 Yes, I do.

 No, I don't.

82

83

1

a basketball player

2

tall   taller   tallest

3

a horse

4

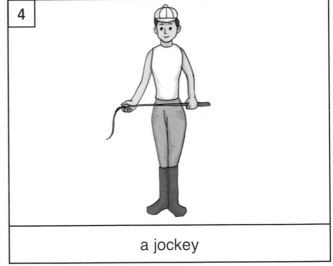

a jockey

5

short   shorter   shortest

1

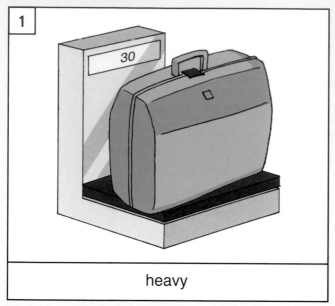

30

heavy

2

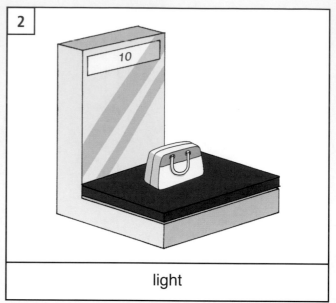

10

light

3

30

heavy

4

35

heavier

5

40

heaviest

6

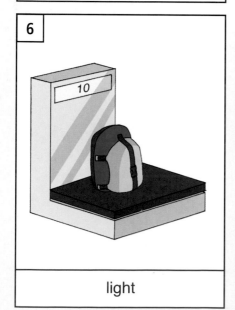

10

light

7

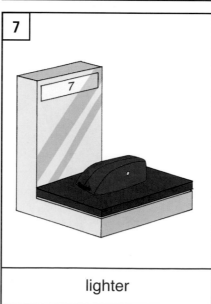

7

lighter

8

5

lightest

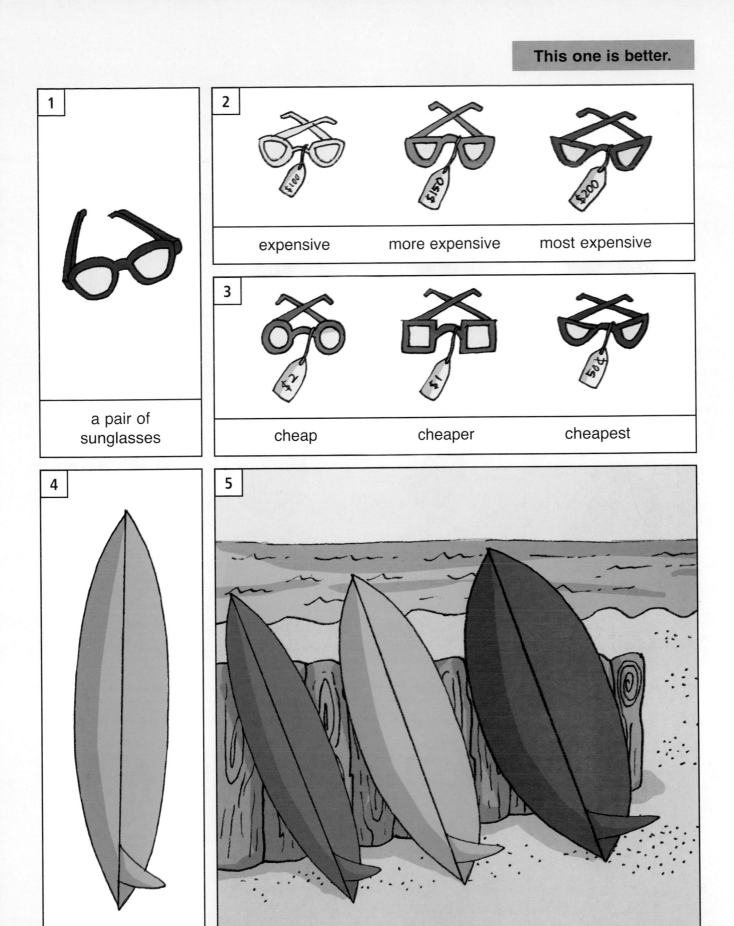

1 a pair of sunglasses

2 expensive | more expensive | most expensive

3 cheap | cheaper | cheapest

4 a surfboard

5 wide | wider | widest

87

1

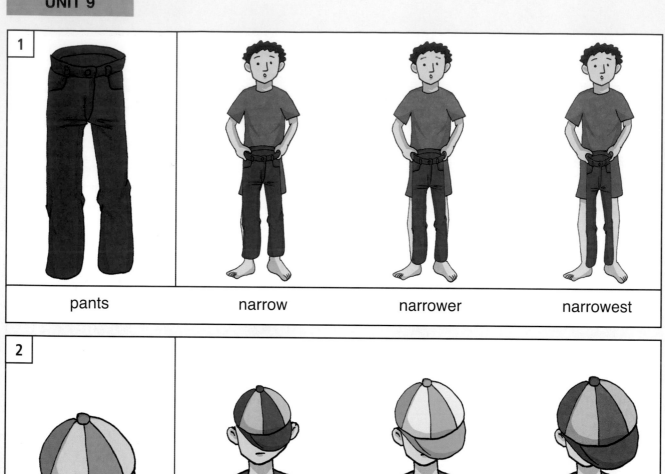

| pants | narrow | narrower | narrowest |

2

| a cap | big | bigger | biggest |

3

| a cap | small | smaller | smallest |

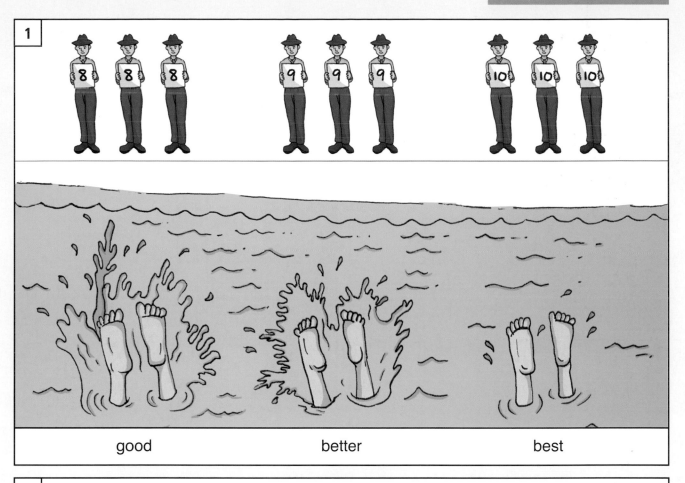

1

good   better   best

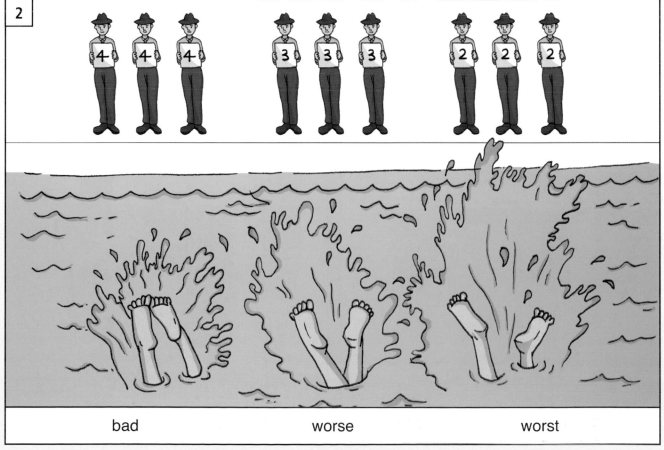

2

bad   worse   worst

The Bensons

UNIT 10: Revision and extension

1. apple
2. ....
3. ....
4. ....
5. ....
6. ....
7. ....
8. ....
9. ....
10. ....
11. ....
12. ....
13. ....
14. ....
15. ....
16. ....
17. ....
18. ....
19. ....
20. ....

21 ....

22 ....

23 ....

24 ....

25 ....

26 ....

27 ....

28 ....

29 ....

30 ....

31 ....

32 ....

33 ....

34 ....

35 ....

36 ....

37 ....

38 ....

39 ....

40 ....

A

1. Would you like a glass of milk?   a. An apple would be nice.

2. She's tall, isn't she?   b. No, I don't.

3. Do you like this restaurant?   c. No, thank you.

4. What would you like?   d. Yes, she is.

B

1. What do you do?   a. He was a police officer.

2. What did you do?   b. I was a teacher.

3. When were you a teacher?   c. From 1991 to 1996.

4. What did your brother do?   d. I'm a taxi driver.

C

1. Where are you from?   a. Three weeks.

2. How long have you been here?   b. Yes, I do.

3. How did you get here?   c. By train.

4. Do you like this hotel?   d. I'm from Tokyo.

D

1. This watch is expensive.   a. This one is bigger.

2. This house is big.   b. This one is more expensive.

3. Those books are cheap.   c. Alan runs faster.

4. Max runs fast.   d. These are cheaper.

Can	eat	glass of	piece of	something	like

can't	take	too	I	you	your

1

Can ....I.... have your tickets, please?

Sure.

2

Are those .... suitcases?

Yes, and this surfboard is ours, ...

3

Can .... put them here, please?

OK.

4

Can I .... my surfboard on the plane?

I'm sorry. You ....

5

Thank you.

about   most   heavier   isn't it   Sure   do   looks   me

1 Excuse ....me......

Yes, can I help you?

2 Yes, thanks. I'd like to look at these laptops.

....

3 This is the lightest.

But it's the .... expensive, isn't it?

Yes, but it's the best.

4 This one is cheaper, ... ?

Yes, but it's bigger and ....

5 How .... this one? It's light, small and not the most expensive.

6 What .... you think?

It .... good.

97

think   by   long   from   much   since   here   For   agree

1

Hotel San Francisco

How long have you been in San Francisco?

For a week.

I've been here since Saturday.

2

How did you get .... ?

I came .... bus from Los Angeles on Thursday.

3

How .... were you in Los Angeles?

.... three days.

4

What do you .... of this hotel?

I like it very .... I think it's great.

I ....

5

Hotel San Francisco

Where do you come ....?

Seoul.

I'm from Sydney. I've been in the USA .... the sixth of July.

1

Would you like something to eat?

➤ to something you eat Would like

➤ be nice chips Some would

2

....?

➤ cup you coffee Would a of like

➤ please Yes

3

....?

➤ here you long have How been

➤ months two For

4

....?

➤ here been How you long have

➤ seventeenth Since September of the

5

....?

TICKETS

➤ get did you here How

➤ taxi By

6

....?

➤ from Where you are

➤ San Francisco from I'm

1

➤ Los Angeles of What think you do

➤ I interesting is think more San Francisco

2

➤ is suitcase This heavier

➤ this one bigger Yes is but

3

➤ ????????????????????????????????

➤ sorry that repeat Could please I'm you

4

➤ like movie you the Did

➤ boring No was It

5

➤ cake like you Do

➤ much Yes very I it like

6

➤ you do do What

➤ manager a I'm

UNIT 10: Answers

Unit 10, page 92

1. apple	2. bag	3. banana	4. cookie
5. beans	6. chips	7. tomatoes	8. cucumber
9. peach	10. plum	11. suitcase	12. nurse
13. bottle of orange juice	14. nuts	15. orange	16. piece of cake
17. sandwich	18. peas	19. cap	20. tablets

Unit 10, page 93

21. ticket	22. lettuce	23. onions	24. bread
25. doctor	26. teacher	27. mechanic	28. police officer
29. receptionist	30. sales assistants	31. taxi driver	32. tea
33. bus	34. train	35. burger	36. socks
37. sausage	38. mushrooms	39. pair of sunglasses	40. carrots

Unit 10, page 94

A. 1c 2d 3b 4a
B. 1d 2b 3c 4a
C. 1d 2a 3c 4b
D. 1b 2a 3d 4c

Unit 10, page 95

1. something
2. piece of, glass of
3. Can
4. like
5. eat

Unit 10, page 96

1. I
2. your, too
3. you
4. take, can't

Unit 10, page 97

1. me
2. Sure
3. most
4. isn't it, heavier
5. about
6. do, looks

Unit 10, page 98

2. here, by
3. long, For
4. think, much, agree
5. from, since

Unit 10, page 99

1. Would you like something to eat?
   Some chips would be nice.

2. Would you like a cup of coffee?
   Yes, please.

3. How long have you been here?
   For two months.

4. How long have you been here?
   Since the seventeenth of September.

5. How did you get here?
   By taxi.

6. Where are you from?
   I'm from San Francisco.

Unit 10, page 100

1 What do you think of Los Angeles?
   I think San Francisco is more interesting.

2. This suitcase is heavier.
   Yes, but this one is bigger.

3. I'm sorry. Could you repeat that please?

4. Did you like the movie?
   No. It was boring.

5. Do you like cake?
   Yes. I like it very much.

6. What do you do?
   I'm a manager.

UNIT 11: What's the matter?

Are you all right? [a:r ju: ɔ:l rait]

What's the matter? [wʌts ðə mæt'ə:r]

What's wrong? [wʌts rɔ:ŋ]

Sorry. [sa:r'ɪ:]

I'm sorry to hear that. [aim sa:r'ɪ: tu: hi:r ðæt]

Thanks for coming. [θæŋks fɔ:r kʌm'iŋ]

hurts [hə:rts]

headache [hed'eik]

backache [bæk'eik]

stomachache [stʌm'əkeik]

earache [i:r'eik]

toothache [tu:θ'eik]

Keep right. [ki:p rait]

back [bæk]

ear [i:r]

foot [fut]

hand [hænd]

head [hed]

knee [ni:]

leg [leg]

arm [a:rm]

shoulder [ʃoul'də:r]

stomach [stʌm'ək]

tooth [tu:θ]

go home [gou houm]

have to [hæv tu:]

pay [pei]

stop [sta:p]

take [teik]

sun [sʌn]

moon [mu:n]

stars [sta:rz]

Good morning. [gud mɔ:r'niŋ]

Good afternoon. [gud æftə:rnu:n']

Good evening. [gud i:v'niŋ]

Good night. [gud nait]

Goodbye. [gudbai']

Bye. [bai]

See you later. [si: ju: lei'tə:r]

Have a nice day. [hæv ə nais dei]

morning [mɔ:r'niŋ]

afternoon [æftə:rnu:n']

evening [i:v'niŋ]

night [nait]

day [dei]

bill [bil]

Dad [dæd]

morning + afternoon + evening + night = 1 day

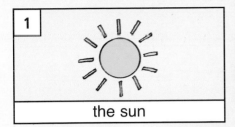
1

the sun

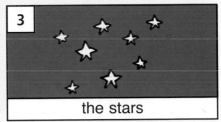
2

the moon

3

the stars

4

morning

5

afternoon

6

7

8

evening

9

night

10

11

103

John is = John's

John's coming.

John's going.

1
head

2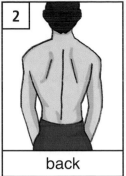
back

3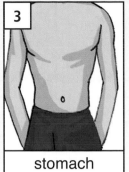
stomach

4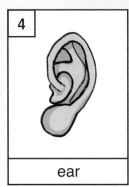
ear

5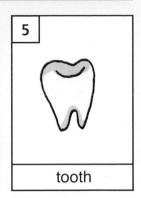
tooth

6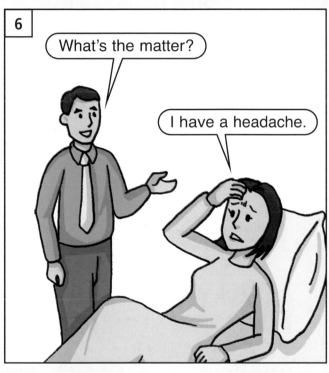

7

8

9

10

1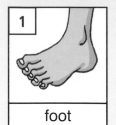
foot

2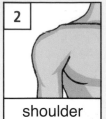
shoulder

3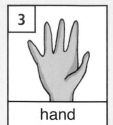
hand

4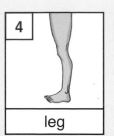
leg

5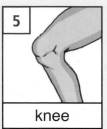
knee

6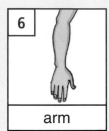
arm

7

8

9

10

11

12

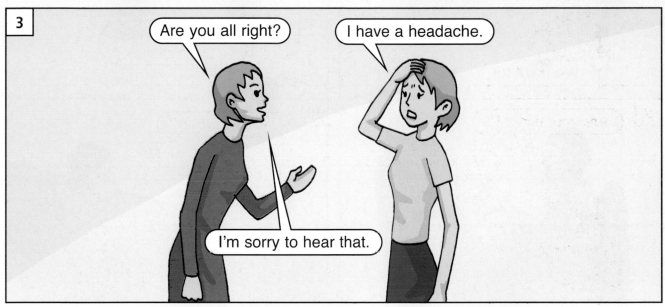

The Bensons

UNIT 12: I live In the big house.

Where do you live? [we:r du: ju: liv]
What's your address? [wʌts ju:r ədres']

I live at... [ai liv æt]

call [kɔ:l]
get [get]

I'll [ail]
will [wil]

hospital [ha:s'pitəl]
police station [pəli:s' stei'ʃən]

near [ni:r]
next door [nekst dɔ:r]
next to [nekst tu:]
opposite [a:p'əzit]
at [æt]
on [a:n]

corner [kɔ:r'nə:r]
around the corner [əraund' ðə kɔ:r'nə:r]
on the corner [a:n ðə kɔ:r'nə:r]

street [stri:t]
road [roud]

address [ədres']
card [ka:rd]

twenty-one [twen'ti: wʌn]
twenty-two [twen'ti: tu:]]
twenty-three [twen'ti: θri:]]
twenty-four [twen'ti: fɔ:r]
twenty-five [twen'ti: faiv]]
twenty-six [twen'ti: siks]
twenty-seven [twen'ti: sev'ən]
twenty-eight [twen'ti: eit]
twenty-nine [twen'ti: nain]
thirty [ðə:r'ti:]

thirty-one [ðə:r'ti: wʌn]
forty [fɔ:r'ti:]
fifty [fif'ti:]
sixty [siks'ti:]
seventy [sev'ən ti:]
eighty [ei'ti:]
ninety [nain'ti:]
one hundred [wʌn hun'drid]
two hundred and one
[tu: hun'drid ænd wʌn]

113

21	22	23	24	25
twenty-one	twenty-two	twenty-three	twenty-four	twenty-five

26	27	28	29	30
twenty-six	twenty-seven	twenty-eight	twenty-nine	thirty

31	**40**	**50**	**60**	**70**
thirty-one	forty	fifty	sixty	seventy

80	**90**	**100**	**200**	**201**
eighty	ninety	one hundred	two hundred	two hundred and one

115

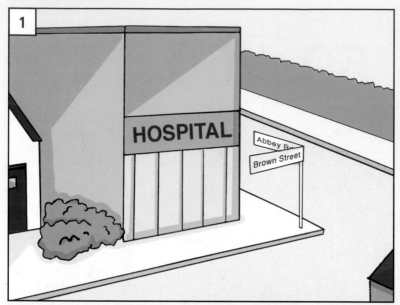

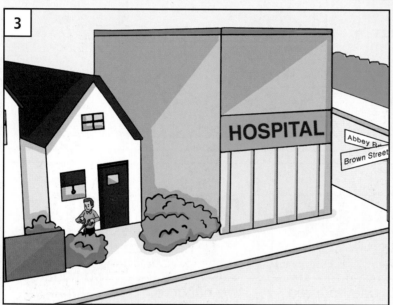

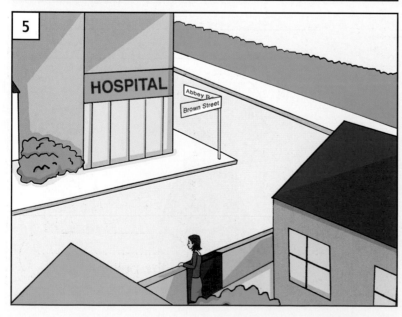

117

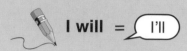

The Bensons

Do [du:]

Do you take... ? [du: ju: teik]

Do you have... ? [du: ju: hæv]

cash [kæʃ]

credit card [kred'it ka:rd]

some [sʌm]

any [en'ɪ:]

How's your ... now? [hauz ju:r ... nau]

You should ... [ju: ʃu:d]

No problem. [nou pra:b'ləm]

That's okay. [ðæts oukei']

play [plei]

piano [pi:æn'ou]

guitar [gita:r']

trumpet [trʌm'pit]

violin [vaiəlin']

or [ɔ:r]

drugstore [drʌg'stɔ:r]

bag [bæg]

tube [tu:b]

carton [ka:r'tən]

box [ba:ks]

egg [eg]

toothpaste [tu:θ'peist]

toothbrush [tu:θ'brʌʃ]

window [win'doʊ]

door [dɔ:r]

floor [flɔ:r]

ceiling [si:'liŋ]

wall [wɔ:l]

room [ru:m]

waiting room [wei'tiŋ ru:m]

make [meik]

need [ni:d]

wait [weit]

old [ould]

new [nu:]

1

I play the piano.

2

He's playing the piano.

3

I play the violin.

4

She's playing the violin.

5

I play the trumpet.

6

He's playing the trumpet.

7

I play the guitar.

8

She's playing the guitar.

1

I …………….. the trumpet.

2

………………… the trumpet?

3

Yes, ………… .

4

I …………….. guitar.

5

………………… guitar?

6

Yes, …………..

7

I …………….. piano.

8

………………… piano?

9

Yes, …………..

1

an old car

2

a new car

3

He needs a new car.

4

an old pair of shoes

5

a new pair of shoes

6

He needs a new pair of shoes.

7

a ticket

8

You need a ticket.

TICKETS

1

I have some nuts.

2

Do you have any nuts?

3

No, I don't have any nuts.

4

I have some cash.

some cash

5

Do you have any cash?

6

No, I don't have any cash.

7

I have some orange juice.

8

.... orange juice?

9

No, ... orange juice.

131

some cash   a credit card

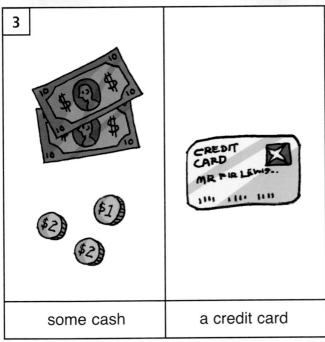

1 — stop

2 — wait

3 — go

4

Wait for me.

5

Let's wait for him.

Sure. We'll wait.

6

Thanks for waiting.

That's okay.

No problem.

7

Ceiling

Wall

Window

Door

Floor

a room

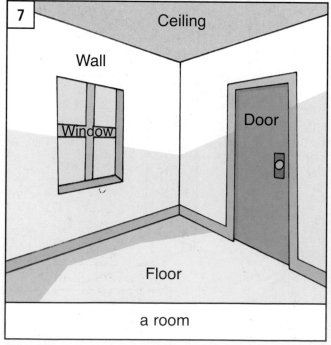

8

Dr. John

a waiting room

134

how is = how's

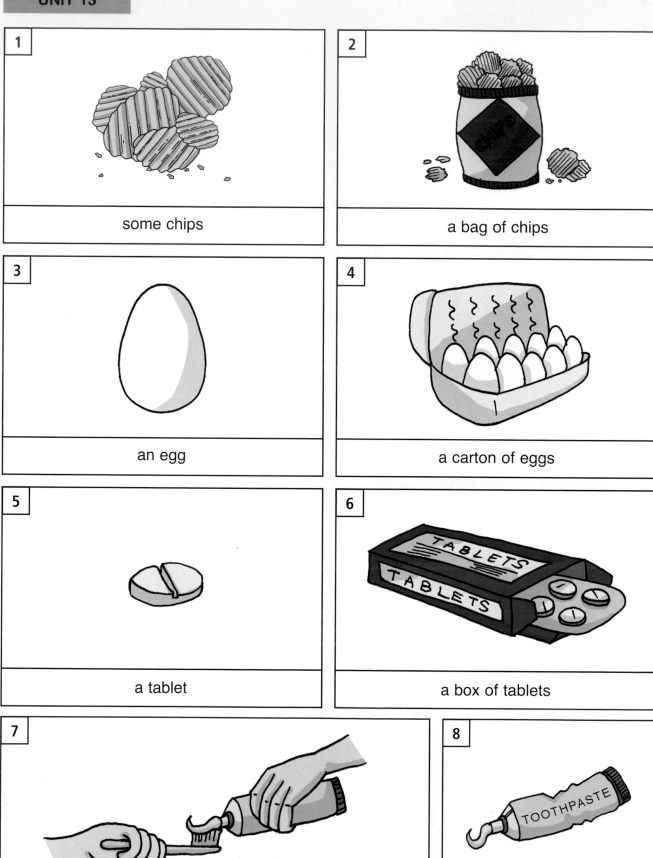

1 some chips

2 a bag of chips

3 an egg

4 a carton of eggs

5 a tablet

6 a box of tablets

7 a toothbrush   some toothpaste

8 a tube of toothpaste

The Bensons

138

UNIT 14: It's the second street on the left.

left   [left]
right   [rait]
straight ahead   [streit əhed']
turn   [tə:rn]

before   [bifɔ:r']
past   [pæst]
with   [wiθ]

bank   [bæŋk]
bus stop   [bʌs sta:p]
cinema   [sin'əmə]
car park   [ka:r pa:rk]
taxi rank   [tæksi: ræŋk]
post office   [poust ɔ:f'is]
gas station   [gæs stei'ʃən]
railway station   [reil'wei stei'ʃən]
supermarket   [su:'pə:rma:rkit]
stadium   [stei'di:əm]
traffic lights   [træf'ik laits]
toilet   [tɔɪ'lit]

first   [fə:rst]
second   [sek'ənd]
third   [θə:rd]
fourth   [fɔ:rθ]
fifth   [fifθ]
sixth   [siksθ]
seventh   [sev'ənθ]
eighth   [eitθ]
ninth   [nainθ]
tenth   [tenθ]

red   [red]
yellow   [jel'ou]
blue   [blu:]
green   [gri:n]
white   [wait]
black   [blæk]
orange   [ɔ:r'indʒ]
brown   [braun]

fence   [fens]
roof   [ru:f]

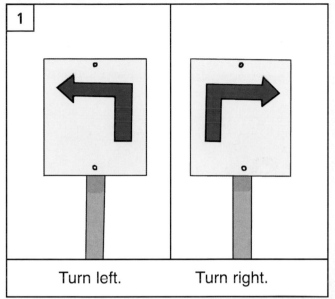

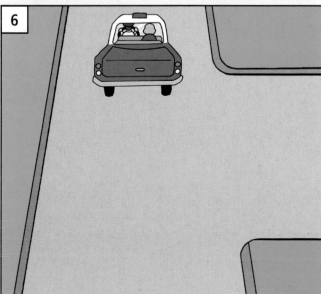

Second   First   Third

first street on the left

second strect on the left

second street on the right

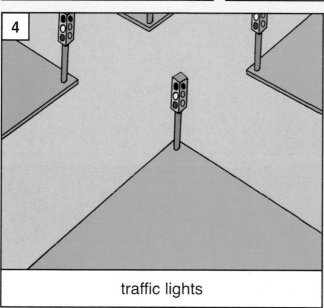

traffic lights

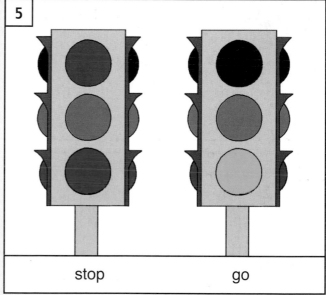

stop   go

before the traffic lights

at the traffic lights

past the traffic lights

Excuse me, where's the...?

1
gas station

2
hospital

3
post office

4
cinema

5
stadium

6
bank

7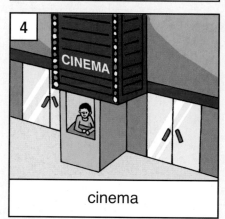
supermarket

8
taxi rank

9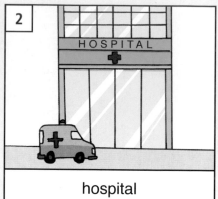
railway station

10
bus stop

11
toilet

12
car park

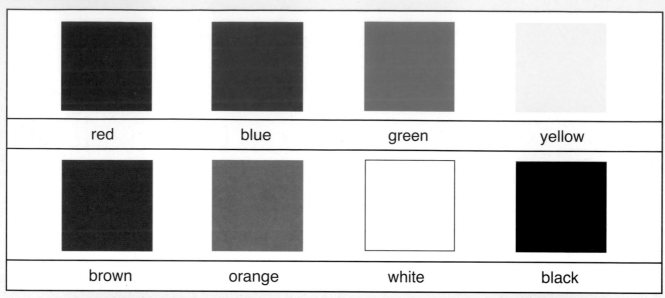

| red | blue | green | yellow |

| brown | orange | white | black |

1

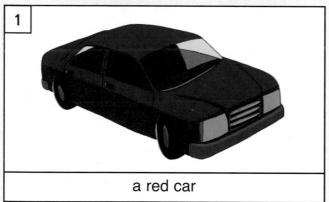

a red car

2

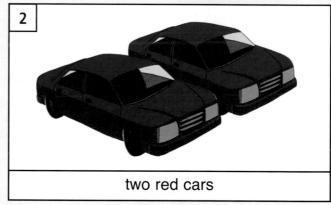

two red cars

3

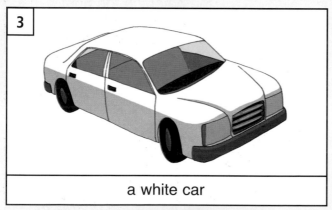

a white car

4

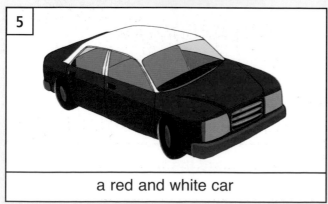

two white cars

5

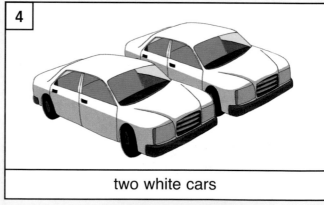

a red and white car

6

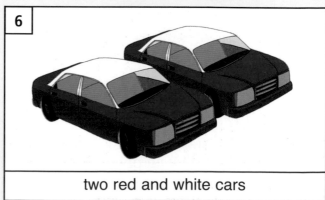

two red and white cars

1

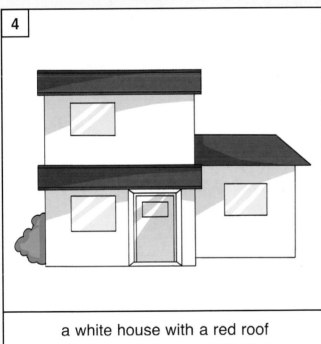

a house

2

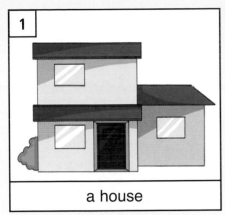

a roof

3

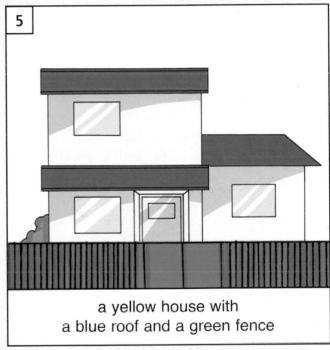

a fence

4

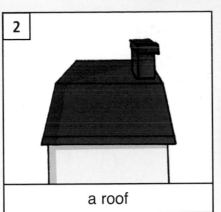

a white house with a red roof

5

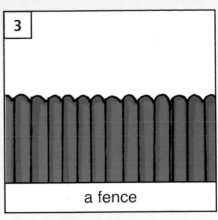

a yellow house with
a blue roof and a green fence

6

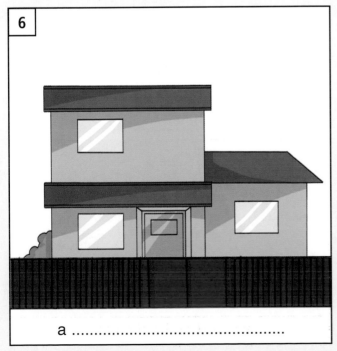

a ....

7

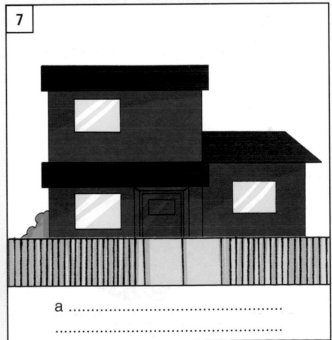

a ....

....

149

The Bensons

1

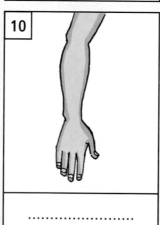

hand
....

2

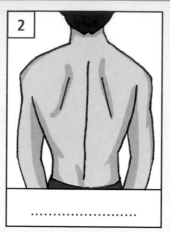

....

3

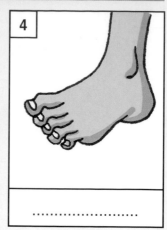

....

4

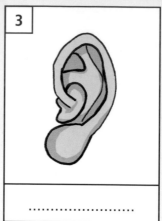

....

5

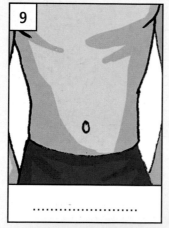

....

6

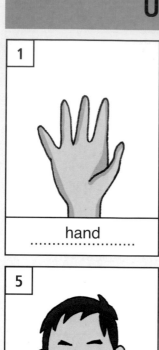

....

7

....

8

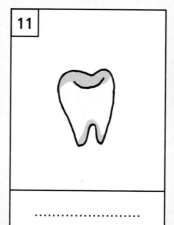

....

9

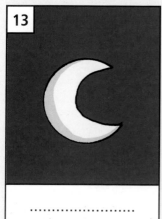

....

10

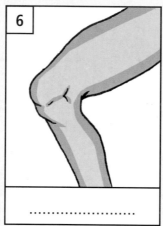

....

11

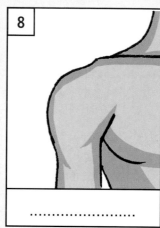

....

12

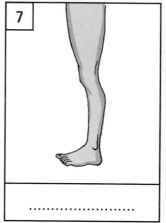

....

13

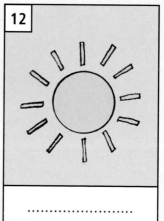

....

14

....

15

....

16

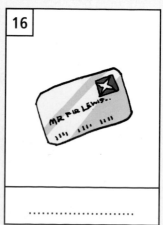

....

17

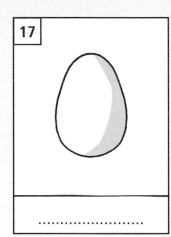

....

18

22 Harden Road

....

19

....

20

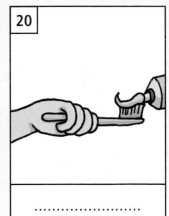

....

21

....

22

....

23

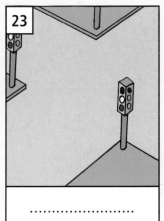

....

24

....

25

....

26

....

27

....

28

....

29

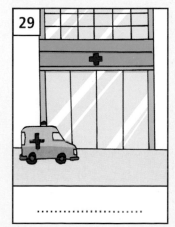

....

30

....

31

....

32

....

A

1. Good morning.

2. What's the matter?

3. I have a headache.

4. How's your headache?

5. Where do you live?

6. What's your address?

a. At 2 Richmond Street.

b. Better, thanks.

c. Good morning.

d. It's 2 Richmond Street.

e. I have a headache.

f. I'm sorry to hear that.

B

1. How's your headache now?

2. How much is this?

3. How much are they?

4. Cash or credit?

5. Are you all right?

6. Where's the hospital?

a. It's ten dollars.

b. My arm hurts

c. Credit, please.

d. It's straight ahead on the left.

e. They're five dollars.

f. Much better, thanks.

C

1. Do we have any apples?

2. Do you play the violin?

3. Do I need a ticket?

4. Does she have any cash?

5. Does he play the trumpet?

6. Do they have a new car?

a. Yes, she does.

b. Yes, we do.

c. No, they don't.

d. Yes, he does.

e. No, I don't.

f. Yes, you do.

hurt	take	chemist	since	evening	at	how	for	have

1

2

3

4

5

6

155

repeat   lights   ahead   left   lights   tell   right   left   help   ahead

live   I'll   How's   My   for   right   with

1

➢ wrong What's

➢ shoulder hurts My.

2

➢ matter the What's

➢ headache a have I

3

➢ I to go now have

➢ a What pity

4

➢ you do Where live

➢ 41 Wik Street live I at

5

➢ me the car where's park Excuse

➢ Sorry know don't I

6

➢ bank the Where's

➢ corner It's the around

➤ ticket need a You

➤ much How it is

➤ I you help Can

➤ these How Yes much shoes are

➤ now your tooth How's

➤ thanks Better

➤ take Do Visa you

➤ Sure

➤ go We now to have

➤ taxi a I'll call

➤ you me waiting for for Thank

➤ OK That's

UNIT 15: Answers

Unit 15, page 152

1. hand	2. back	3. ear	4. foot
5. head	6. knee	7. leg	8. shoulder
9. stomach	10. arm	11. tooth	12. sun
13. moon	14. stars	15. cash	16. credit card

Unit 15, page 153

17. egg	18. address	19. window	20. toothbrush
21. taxi rank	22. toilet	23. traffic lights	24. gas station
25. waiting room	26. bank	27. bus stop	28. cinema
29. hospital	30. police station	31. post office	32. railway station

Unit 15, page 154

A. 1c 2e 3f 4b 5a 6d   B. 1f 2a 3e 4c 5b 6d   C. 1b 2e 3f 4a 5d 6c

Unit 15, page 155

2. how, have   3. Since   4. hurt   5. take, for, evening   6. at, chemist

Unit 15, page 156

1. help   3. left, lights, ahead, repeat   4. left, lights, ahead, right

Unit 15, page 157

1. Where   2. much   3. look   4. next   5. take   6. like

Unit 15, page 158

1. right, My   3. I'll   4. live, with   5. for   6. How's

Unit 15, page 159

1. What's wrong?
   My shoulder hurts.

2. What's the matter?
   I have a headache.

3. I have to go now.
   What a pity.

4. Where do you live?
   I live at 41 Wik Street.

5. Excuse me, where's the car park?
   Sorry, I don't know.

6. Where's the bank?
   It's around the corner.

Unit 15, page 160

1. You need a ticket.
   How much is it?

2. Can I help you?
   Yes. How much are these shoes?

3. How's your tooth now?
   Better, thanks.

4. Do you take Visa?
   Sure.

5. We have to go now.
   I'll call a taxi.

6. Thank you for waiting for me.
   That's OK.

UNIT 16: She bought a cake.

wash   [wɔ:ʃ]

pull   [pul]

push   [puʃ]

open   [ouˈpən]

close   [klouz]

talk   [tɔ:k]

write   [rait]

sleep   [sli:p]

buy   [bai]

sell   [sel]

drive   [draiv]

eat   [i:t]

teach   [ti:tʃ]

Mum   [ma:m]

was   [wʌz]

were   [wə:r]

clean   [kli:n]

dirty   [də:rˈti:]

it will = it'll   **he will =** he'll   **she will =** she'll

turn	turning	turned
play	playing	played
call	calling	called
work	working	worked
arrive	arriving	arrived
agree	agreeing	agreed
wait	waiting	waited
stop	stopping	stopped

1

It'll turn right.

2

It's turning right.

3
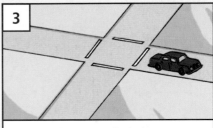
It turned right.

4

He'll play the piano.

5

He's playing the piano.

6

He played the piano.

7

She'll call him.

8

She's calling him.

9

She called him.

wash	washing	washed
open	opening	opened
close	closing	closed
pull	pulling	pulled
push	pushing	pushed
talk	talking	talked

1

He's washing the car.

2

He's opening the door.

3

He's closing the door.

4

They're pulling the car.

5

They're pushing the car.

6

She's talking to him.

1

He'll pull the suitcase.

2

He's .... the suitcase.

3

He pulled the suitcase.

4

.... his hands.

5

He's washing his hands.

6

He .... his hands.

7

She'll close the window.

8

.... the window.

9

.... the window.

165

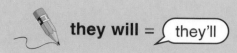 they will = they'll

run	running	ran
eat	eating	ate
bring	bringing	brought
come	coming	came
go	going	went
take	taking	took
do	doing	did
meet	meeting	met
have	having	had
leave	leaving	left
think	thinking	thought
pay	paying	paid
hurt	hurting	hurt
get	getting	got
make	making	made
teach	teaching	taught

1 He'll run.

2 He's running.

3 He ran.

4 They'll eat them.

5 They're eating them.

6 They ate them.

166

sleep	sleeping	slept
write	writing	wrote
buy	buying	bought
sell	selling	sold
drive	driving	drove

1

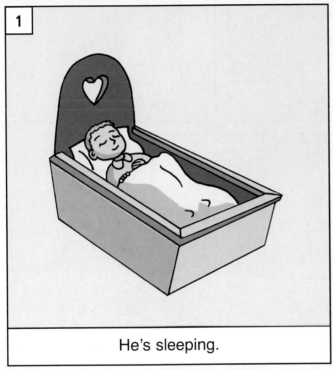

He's sleeping.

2

She's writing.

3

She's buying a ticket.
He's selling a ticket.

4

He's driving a car.

1

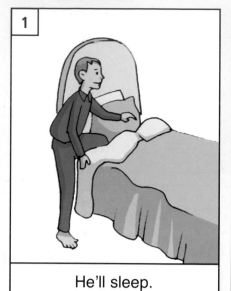

He'll sleep.

2

He's sleeping.

3

He ....

4

She'll teach them.

5

.... them.

6

She .... them.

7

.... a cake.

8

She's buying a cake.

9

She .... a cake.

I am	I was
You are	You were
He is	He was
She is	She was
It is	It was
We are	We were
They are	They were

1

It's a yellow house.

2

3

It was a yellow house.
Now it's a red house.

4

They're clean cars.

5

6

They were clean cars.
Now they're dirty cars.

The Bensons

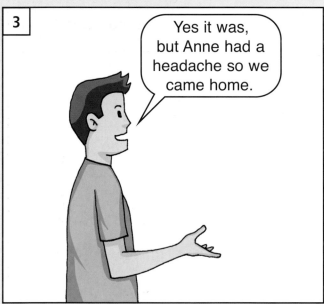

read [ri:d]

watch [wa:tʃ]

work [wə:rk]

swim [swim]

shop [ʃa:p]

drink [driŋk]

newspaper [nu:zʹpeipə:r]

television [telʹəvɪʒən]

garden [ga:rdən]

play [plei]

chess [tʃes]

football [futʹbɔ:l]

golf [ga:lf]

tennis [tenʹis]

telephone (phone) [telʹəfoun]

I'll get it. [ail get it]

speak [spi:k]

Who's calling? [hu:z kɔ:lʹiŋ]

ask [æsk]

message [mesʹidʒ]

leave a message [li:v ə mesʹidʒ]

take a message [teik ə mesʹidʒ]

hair [he:r]

have a haircut [hæv ə he:rʹkʌt]

number [numʹbə:r]

beep [bi:p]

busy [bizi:]

please [pli:z]

after [æfʹtə:r]

before [bifɔ:rʹ]

long [lɔ:ŋ]

short [ʃɔ:rt]

full [ful]

empty [emʹti:]

breakfast [brekʹfəst]

lunch [lʌntʃ]

dinner [dinʹə:r]

1	2	3
 a piano		
4	5	6
 a newspaper		
7	8	9
 a garden		

1

washing the car

2

Do you like washing the car?

3

Yes, I do.

No, I don't.

4

swimming

5

Do your children like swimming?

6

Yes, they do.

7

reading

8

Do you like reading?

9

Yes, I do. Reading is interesting.

No, I don't. It's boring.

1

driving the car

2

Do you like ....?

3

....

4

shopping

5

Does your husband ....?

6

....

7

watching television

8

Do you like ....?

9

Yes, ... interesting.

No, ... boring.

1

a dirty car

2

a clean car

3

before washing
the car

4

washing the car

5

after washing
the car

6

long hair

7

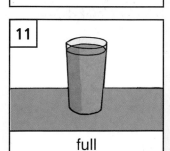

short hair

8

before having
a haircut

9

having a haircut

10

after having
a haircut

11

full

12

empty

13

....
drinking the
orange juice

14

drinking the
orange juice

15

....
drinking the
orange juice

1

a telephone

I'll get it.

Hello. John speaking.

2

Excuse me.

Hello. John speaking.

3

Can you get it, David? I'm busy.

Sure.

Hello. John's phone. David speaking.

breakfast

lunch

dinner

before dinner

after dinner

a message

leaving a message

taking a message

a telephone

179

1 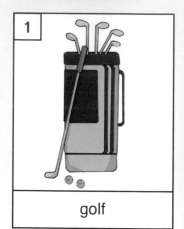 golf	**2**  He's playing golf.	**3**  He was playing golf.
4  tennis	**5**  They're playing tennis.	**6** 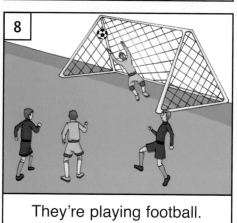 They were playing tennis.
7 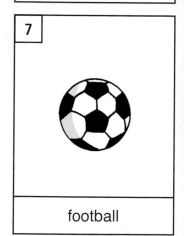 football	**8**  They're playing football.	**9**  They were playing football.
10  chess	**11**  They're playing chess.	**12**  They were playing chess.

The Bensons

184

Can you tell me the time, please?
[kæn ju: tel mi: ðə taim pli:z]

What's the time? [wʌtz ðə taim]

clock [kla:k]

quarter [kwɔ:r'tə:r]
half [hæf]

o'clock [əkla:k']
a quarter past [ə kwɔ:r'tə:r pæst]
half past [hæf pæst]
a quarter to [ə kwɔ:r'tə:r tu:]

a.m. [ei em]
p.m. [pi: em]

appointment [əpɔint'mənt]
flight [flait]
wedding [wed'iŋ]

angry [æŋ'gri:]
happy [hæp'i:]
sad [sæd]
worried [wə:ri:d]

welcome [wel'kəm]

yesterday [jes'tə:rdei]
today [tədei']
tomorrow [təmɔ:r'ou]

early [ə:r'li:]
late [leit]

1

some clocks

2

one o'clock

3

two o'clock

4

three o'clock

5

one o'clock

6

two o'clock

7

three o'clock

8

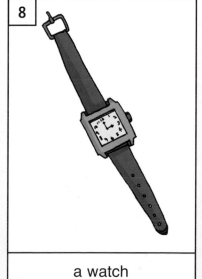

a watch

9

What's the time, please?

It's two o'clock.

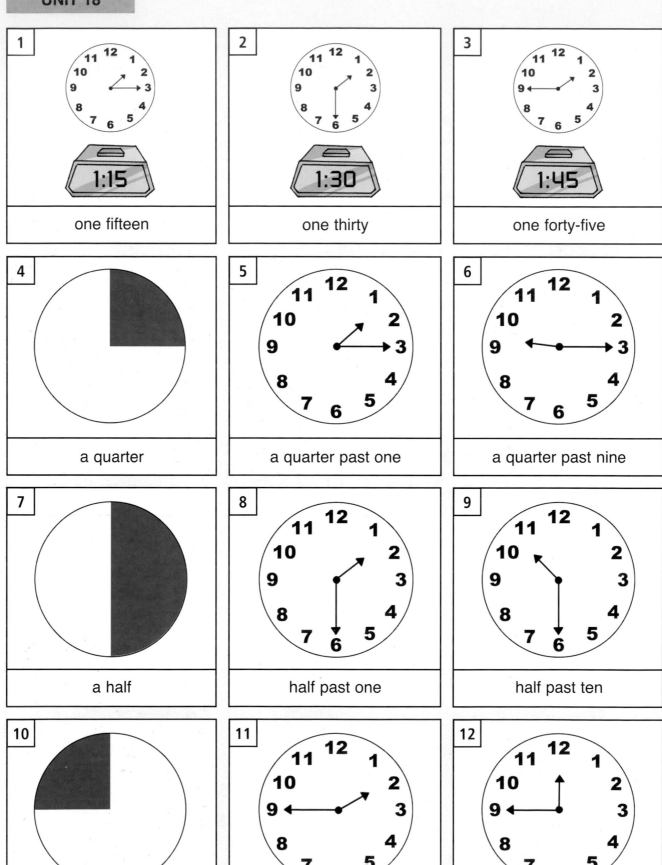

1 one fifteen

2 one thirty

3 one forty-five

4 a quarter

5 a quarter past one

6 a quarter past nine

7 a half

8 half past one

9 half past ten

10 a quarter

11 a quarter to two

12 a quarter to twelve

1

Can you tell me the time, please?

It's a quarter past five.

2

Can you tell me the time, please?

It's half past five.

3

Can you tell me the time, please?

It's a quarter to six.

4

....
....
....

....
....

5

....
....
....

....
....

6

....
....
....

....
....

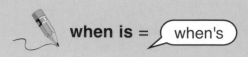

when is = when's

1

When's the meeting?

At half past ten.

2

When does the train leave?

TIMETABLE
2:45

At a quarter to three.

3	4	5	6	7
	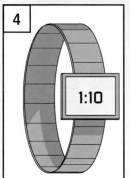	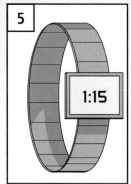	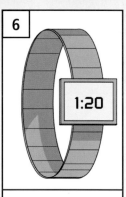	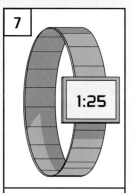
1:05	1:10	1:15	1:20	1:25
five past one	ten past one	a quarter past one	twenty past one	twenty-five past one
one o five	one ten	one fifteen	one twenty	one twenty-five

8	9	10	11	12
	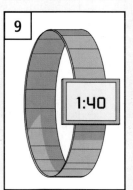	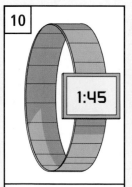	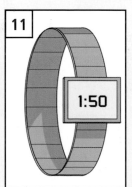	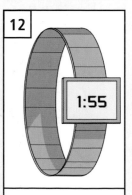
1:35	1:40	1:45	1:50	1:55
twenty-five to two	twenty to two	quarter to two	ten to two	five to two
one thirty-five	one forty	one forty-five	one fifty	one fifty-five

7:05 a.m.

7:05 p.m.

a wedding

When's the wedding?

It's at two thirty tomorrow.

When's the wedding?

It's at two thirty today.

When's the wedding?

It was at two thirty yesterday.

193

1. She's happy.

2. She's sad.

3. She's worried.

4. She's angry.

5. She's very happy.

6. She's very sad.

7. She's .... worried.

8. She's .... angry.

Mary's waiting for her husband. He's late.

He's very late and she's angry.

The Bensons

Does this bus go to... ?   [dʌz ðis bʌs gou tu:]

Can you tell me when to get off
[kæn ju: tel mi: wen tu: get ɔ:f]

How long... ?   [hau lɔ:ŋ]

timetable   [taim'teibəl]

bicycle   [bai'sikəl]

ferry   [fe:r'i:]

tram   [træm]

heat   [hi:t]

miss   [mis]

use   [ju:z]

park   [pa:rk]

heated   [hi:t'id]

missed   [mist]

used   [ju:zd]

parked   [pa:rkt]

second   [sek'ənd]

minute   [min'it]

hour   [au'ə:r]

You're not allowed to...
[ju:r na:t əlau'd tu:]

No parking   [nou pa:rkiŋ]

get off   [get ɔ:f]

get on   [get a:n]

change   [tʃeindʒ]

Here you are.   [hi:r ju: a:r]

a bus	He's waiting for the bus.

He's getting on the bus.	He's going by bus.

She missed the bus.	He's getting off the bus.

1 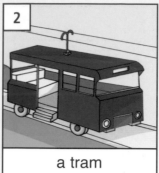 a train	**2**  a tram	**3**  a plane	**4** 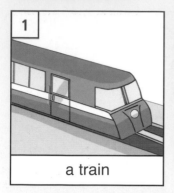 a ferry

5

She .... the ferry.

6

She's getting off ....

7

They're .... by tram.

8

....
....

9

....
....

10

....
....

1

one hour

2

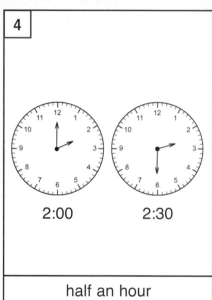

The meeting is in one hour.

3

How long will it take?

Two hours.

4

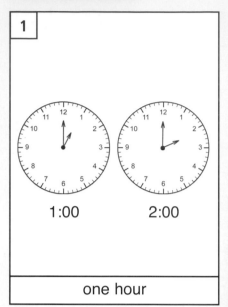

half an hour

5

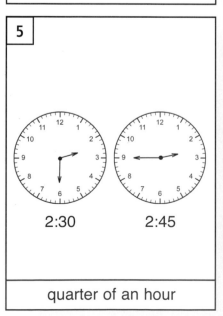

quarter of an hour

6

DEPARTURES
4:30 NEW YORK

When does the plane for New York leave?

In half an hour.

1

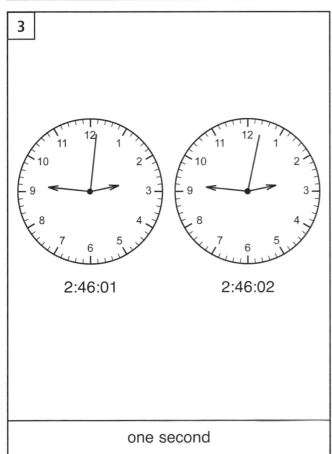

2:45   2:46

one minute

2

3

2:46:01   2:46:02

one second

4

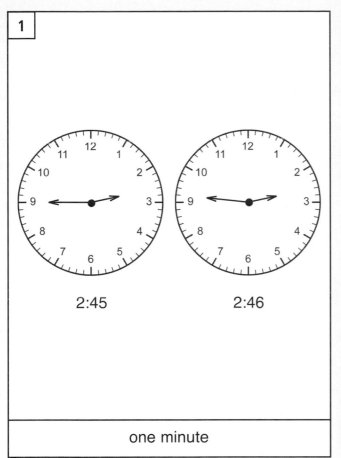

1

a timetable

2

Do you have a timetable, please?

Sure, here you are.

Thanks.

3

When's the next train to Hawthorn?

In ten minutes.

4

How long will it take to get there?

Twenty five minutes.

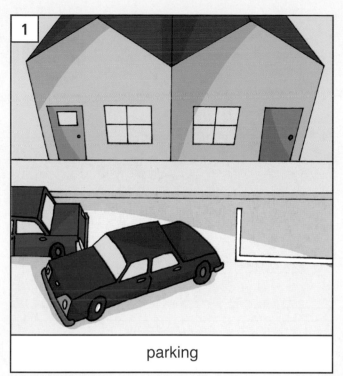

parking

No parking

You're not allowed to park here.

The Bensons

1. Are you going out after lunch?

Yes. I left my credit card at the drugstore and I have to go and get it.

2. Tom's waiting for the bus. He's going to the drugstore in Fenwick Street.

3. Does this bus go to Fenwick street?

No, you missed that bus. The next bus to Fenwick street is in half an hour.

4. Tom's worried. He has to be at the drugstore at 2:30. He'll be late.

5.

6. Does this bus go to Fenwick street?

Yes, it does.

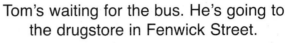

210

1
bicycle
....

2
....

3
....

4
....

5
....

6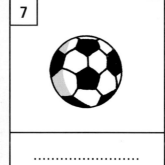
....

7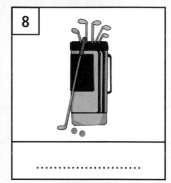
....

8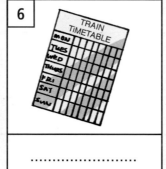
....

9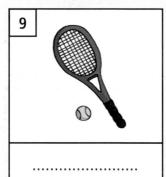
....

10
....

11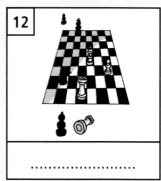
....

12
....

13
....

14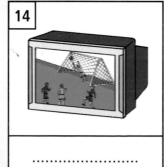
....

15
....

16
....

17
....

18
....

19
....

20
....

A

1. Can I speak to Sue, please?

2. Who's calling?

3. Can I take a message?

4. What's your number?

a. It's 874298.

b. Sorry, she's busy. Can I take a message?

c. This is Peter.

d. Ask her to call me after lunch, please.

B

1. What's the time?

2. When's the appointment?

3. When was the meeting?

4. You're not allowed to park here.

a. Tomorrow at two o'clock.

b. Yesterday at two o'clock.

c. It's two o'clock.

d. Sorry. I didn't know.

C

1. Does this bus go to Crown road?

2. When's the next train?

3. How much to Richmond street?

4. Have you got a timetable?

a. Three dollars twenty.

b. Sure, here you are.

c. At half past four.

d. Yes, it does.

D

1. Does she like playing the piano?

2. Do you like watching television?

3. Does he like playing football?

4. Do they like shopping?

a. No, he doesn't.

b. Yes, they do.

c. No, she doesn't.

d. Yes, I do.

late	message	meet	past	I'll	ten	leave	speaking	time

1

What **time** is it?

Five past two.

Is it? I have a meeting with the accountant. I need to call him.

2

This is John Thompson. I can't answer the phone now. Please .... a .... after the beep - BEEP.

Hello, John. This is Allan. It's .... two. I'm .... for our meeting. Is two thirty okay?

3

.... get it.

4

Allan Smith ....

Hello Allan. This is John. Two thirty is okay.

5

I'll .... you in ten minutes.

Okay.

went   ate   bought   didn't   liked   thought   stayed   for

1

"You went to Australia last year, ... you?"

"Yes, ... three weeks. It was great."

2

We .... in Sydney. We saw the Opera House. I .... it was beautiful.

3

We .... to the beach in the afternoons.

4

"How was the hotel?"

"Great. We .... it very much."

5

We .... at the hotel restaurant every night.

6

We .... some souvenirs.

| lift | room | key | third | names | like | floor | open | watching |

1

Good evening.

Good evening. We'd like a .... for two nights.

2

Sure. Can I have your .... , please?

Paul and Maria Johnson.

3

We'd .... a room with a view of the beach.

No problem.

4

We like .... movies. Does the room have a television?

Yes, it does.

5

You're in room seventy three. Go to the third .... and your room is the .... on the left.

6

Here's your .... The hotel restaurant is .... for dinner. Enjoy your stay.

1

➤ I speak John Can to

➤ him get I'll Sure.

2

➤ the What's time

➤ a seven to It's quarter

3

➤ is the to next When Rockdale train

➤ thirty eleven At five

4

➤ open restaurant does When the

➤ this quarter a seven past evening At

5

➤ meeting the When's

➤ nine morning past At tomorrow half

6

➤ arrive When plane the does

➤ past At half afternoon this two

1

➤ bus go Crown Road this Does to

➤ does Yes it

2

➤ this Queenscliff to go Does train

➤ doesn't No it

3

➤ to much Kingsfield How it is

➤ dollars three It's

4

➤ running like you Do

➤ don't I No

5

➤ driving like you Do

➤ I Yes do

6

➤ allowed You are not park here to

➤ know I Sorry didn't

219

UNIT 20: Answers

Unit 20, page 212

1. bicycle	2. tram	3. breakfast	4. lunch	5. dinner
6. timetable	7. football	8. golf	9. tennis	10. message
11. newspaper	12. chess	13. telephone	14. television	15. wedding
16. clock	17. happy	18. angry	19. worried	20. sad

Unit 20, page 213

A. 1b 2c 3d 4a   B. 1c 2a 3b 4d   C. 1d 2c 3a 4b   D. 1c 2d 3a 4b

Unit 20, page 214

1. time   2. leave, message, ten, past, late   3. I'll   4. speaking   5. meet

Unit 20, page 215

2. At   3. In   4. earlier   5. late, wait   6. next

Unit 20, page 216

1. didn't, for   2. stayed, thought   3. went   4. liked   5. ate   6. bought

Unit 20, page 217

1. room   2. names   3. like   4. watching   5. floor, third   6. key, open

Unit 20, page 218

1. Can I speak to John?
   Sure, I'll get him.

2. What's the time?
   It's a quarter to seven.

3. When's the next train to Rockdale?
   At eleven thirty five.

4. When does the restaurant open?
   At a quarter past seven this evening.

5. When is the meeting?
   At half past nine tomorrow morning.

6. When does the plane arrive?
   At half past two this afternoon.

Unit 20, page 219

1. Does this bus go to Crown Road?
   Yes, it does.

2. Does this train go to Queenscliff?
   No, it doesn't.

3. How much is it to Kingsfield?
   It's three dollars.

4. Do you like running?
   No, I don't.

5. Do you like driving?
   Yes, I do.

6. You are not allowed to park here.
   Sorry, I didn't know.

Index

Notes